HOW TO BE A

FASHION DESIGNER

Written by Lesley Ware

Dolls by Tiki Papier

Author Lesley Ware
Illustrator Tiki Papier

THIS EDITION
Editor Abi Maxwell
Designer Sonny Flynn
US Editor Margaret Parrish
US Senior Editor Shannon Beatty
Managing Editor Gemma Farr
Managing Art Editor Diane Peyton Jones
Production Editor Dragana Puvacic
Production Controller Becky Parton

FIRST EDITION
Editors Satu Fox, Megan Weal
Designers Joanne Clark, Emma Hobson
Managing Editors Deborah Lock, Laura Gilbert
Managing Art Editor Diane Peyton Jones
Production Editor Dragana Puvacic
Production Controller Barbara Ossowska

This American Edition, 2024
First American Edition, 2018
Published in the United States by DK Publishing,
a division of Penguin Random House LLC
1745 Broadway, 20th Floor, New York, NY 10019

A catalog record for this book
is available from the Library of Congress.
ISBN 978-0-5938-4051-1

DK books are available at special discounts when purchased
in bulk for sales promotions, premiums, fund-raising, or
educational use.
For details, contact: DK Publishing Special Markets,
1745 Broadway, 20th Floor, New York, NY 10019
SpecialSales@dk.com

Printed and bound in China
www.dk.com

This book was made with Forest
Stewardship Council™ certified
paper – one small step in DK's
commitment to a sustainable future.
Learn more at **www.dk.com/uk/
information/sustainability**

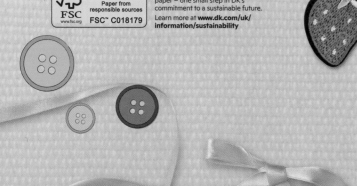

CONTENTS

Drinking tea from my rainbow mug makes me happy when I'm sewing!

Classic black-and-white is my favorite combination.

Hi, I'm Lesley. I write books about fashion, teach sewing classes, and design (all the time).

Hey there, fashion star!

Did you know you're holding a super-cool book that's your pass into the massive world of fashion? It's like a map to a place where clothes are kind to nature and where everyone feels awesome in what they wear.

Creating style is like a giant coloring book, where you get to mix up colors, shapes, lines, textures, and all sorts of materials to show the world who you are!

This is your guide to becoming a fashion detective, hunting for clues on how to make clothes that don't hurt our planet. You'll also learn about natural fabrics, which are better for the environment, so you can bring them into your designs.

Sew, get ready to enter this magical journey of fashion, where you'll create clothes that tell a story, help our planet, and make everyone feel like they belong.

My cat, Miles Ware, dreams of being the first cat on the moonwalk, I mean, the catwalk. He's already practicing his fierce walk and purr-fect poses!

xo, Lesley

Hunt for textiles

Look around for old clothes that don't fit anymore, and fabrics that could be turned into fashion gold! It's like a treasure hunt where you save the planet and make cool stuff at the same time. It's a win-win!

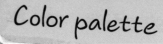

A palette is a set of colors for creating designs. This is a palette of the colors I love most right now.

I enjoy listening to music when I design and sew!

Fashion 4 all

Design with everyone in mind! Think about how your clothes can make anyone feel fabulous, no matter who they are. What can you make that is fashionable and inclusive?

Mix, match, make magic

Try combining colors and patterns that you wouldn't usually see together. It's a fun way to be unique, and you might just start a new trend.

Make it

You'll find great projects throughout the book to help you get started with the practical side of creating real-life fashion.

Where you see this symbol, ask an adult to help you with the activity. ALWAYS ask for help from an adult when cutting and sewing—scissors and needles are sharp.

Don't forget!

There is no such thing as "I can't" or "it's ugly"—work until it feels right. Designing is an art, not a science.

Take your time. Have fun with your projects and see where they take you.

Believe in your ideas and follow your instincts. Now—let's get started!

TOOLS

Here are some tools you will need to do the activities in this book. These items, along with a stash of fabric, are a blast to draw and design with. You can also start a library of fashion books to use as inspiration.

Double-sided tape

Sequins

Mini pom-poms

Embellishing

Embellishing is a big word that simply means "decorating." You can easily make your clothes look completely different with pom-poms or sequins.

Colored pencils

Washi tape

Washi tape is adhesive tape made of paper. Use it to embellish clothes and decorate mood boards.

Fabric paint

Fabric glue

Drawing

Sketching clothes is fun and you will get better and better if you practice every day. Try different-sized sketchbooks and aim to fill the one you like most.

Sketchbooks

Pencil

Crayons

Colored markers

Use thin and thick markers to draw delicate details or chunky stripes.

Scissors

Buttons

Needle

sewing

To start sewing, you just need a needle and thread. As you begin to sew more, you can add more supplies to your kit—keep all of your pins, needles, and buttons in one safe place.

Swatches

Cotton thread

Dressmaker's pins

You can mix dyes to create unique colors.

Fabric pen

Fabric dye

How to do a running stitch

The running stitch is the most common stitch. Think of it as a wave that goes up and down, in and out of the fabric. Remember always to cut and sew **away** from your body, with an adult's help.

Push one end of the thread through the eye of the needle. Tie a knot in the other end of the thread.

1

Patches

2

When you're finished, tie a knot in the thread to stop it from coming loose.

3

Starting from the back, poke the needle through the fabric until the knot stops it. Then poke the needle back through the fabric.

Keep moving the needle forward and backward through the fabric. Try to keep your stitches the same distance apart.

How to
MOOD BOARD

A mood board is a collection of things that you can use for style inspiration. Fashion designers use them to show their ideas to others. Let's spark new ideas with a rainbow mood board.

Find inspiring things

After you grab a pair of scissors, hunt around for items to add to your mood board. Choose images from magazines, favorite photos, stickers, leaves, and fabric. You can pin your inspirational pieces to a bulletin board, stick them to a piece of cardboard, or make a mini-mood board in a sketchbook.

rainbow

Colors

Get started by thinking of a color you like to wear. Look everywhere for inspiration to add to your board, from photos to buttons. Use as many shades of your color as you can find.

Fabric swatches

Pin inspirational items to your board.

Ask for a few fabric swatches the next time you are at a fabric store.

Add small objects such as patches or hair accessories to your mood board.

Keep an eye out for things that remind you of your mood board theme and colors.

Themes

A theme connects images together. Your theme could be a set of objects, such as "cute dogs," or a feeling, such as "joy." Make a mood board with a theme that sends a message about your sense of style.

Bracelets

Magazine cuttings

Tear out inspiring quotes from magazines.

Find your voice as a designer

COLOR

Color is the most important element of design because it's part of every single thing you wear. For each collection, fashion designers create a color palette by picking out a few colors that go together.

Blues are cool and serene. They come in lots of tones, from sky blue to navy.

Purples

Pastel blue

Lilac

Pinks and reds

Pastel pink

Shocking pink

Pastels

Pastels are milky, washed-out tones that create a soothing effect. They are great for spring outfits.

Pistachio green, lilac, and baby blue are all pastels.

Ribbon is a great trim. Buy lengths of ribbon in a mix of colors for different projects.

Blues and black

Designers love black because it goes with everything.

Teal

Mint green

Sunflower yellow

← Red, orange, and yellow colors are warm and bright.

Yellows and greens

← Neon pink is an example of a "bright."

Brights

Brights are strong, bold colors. They are fun to wear and look flashy, especially when you pair at least two together.

Color-code your fabric to easily see different textures and prints.

Top tip

Contrasting colors are opposites on the color wheel. They stand out strongly when you put them together. Try designing a color-blocked outfit in contrasting tones.

Color wheel

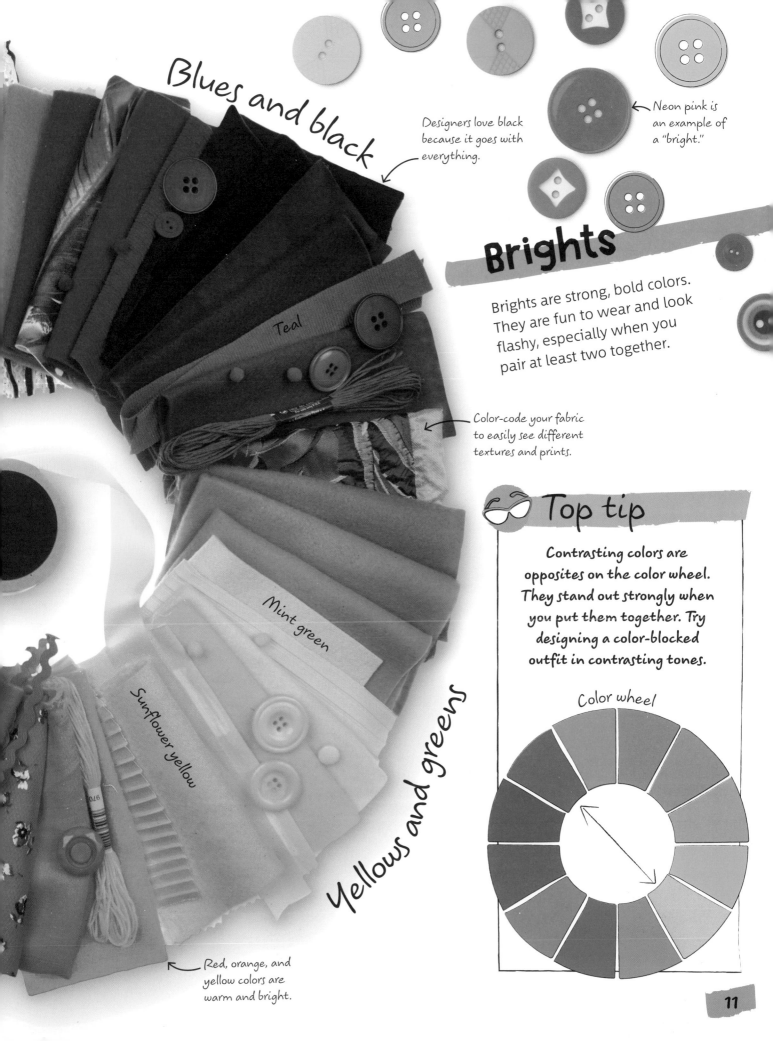

Balloons

Design an outline using the shape of a balloon. Try a ballooning sleeve, dress, or pants.

Deep purple

Green

Bunting

Blue

Ferris wheel

ADMIT ONE

Tickets

Create a new mood board using this carnival color palette.

Cotton candy

Big-top red stripes

At the
CARNIVAL

Carnivals are an unlimited source of inspiration. Pick a carnival-themed word to start your design— think of things like happy, light, star, candy, or neon.

Let the sights, sounds, and even tastes and smells of the carnival inspire you. Can you design a popcorn-inspired look?

Popcorn

Be inspired by the colors and **stripes** of the main tent.

Masquerade mask

Big top

Stars are the symbols of performers.

Cherry red

Cotton-candy pink

Zigzags

Stars

The Look

This look is for the person who is ready to slay all day, checking out the amusements that come their way! No need to be plain when you can look like a star.

A bunting-patterned scarf keeps your hair from blowing around on all the fairground rides.

Big-top **stripes** make a cute T-shirt pattern.

How can you include light in your designs? Consider reflective materials, LED lights, or glow-in-the-dark paints.

Bright lights

This bracelet has chunky sections shaped like fairground **tickets**.

Add studs or gems to your design in a shape you adore.

Juggling pins

Create a cool and quirky look fit for a juggler, but easy to wear every day.

A cuffed jumpsuit looks summery and casual. You can make your own rolled-up cuffs by adding a few stitches.

Wearing comfy shoes is a must at the carnival. You can't have fun if your feet are beat.

Pick a PALETTE

Color is one of the most powerful and popular elements of fashion design. Check out these looks for different ways that designers use color. Then create a personal palette by choosing a set of colors that works well for you.

Confident color-blocking

Dark pants are great for color-blocking because they contrast well with bright, bold colors. →

Challenge

Create a color-blocked, a pastel, and a crazy-color look from pieces you already have in your wardrobe. Lay each outfit on your bed or a clean floor so you can clearly see whether it works or not. This is just the first draft of your look! Keep swapping in items until the look is perfect. Don't forget to include shoes (see pages 34–35) and bags (see pages 24–25).

color-blocking

On your mark, get set, color-block! A color-blocked look means wearing two or more solid-colored pieces of clothing. It's an easy look to achieve—you simply mix one or two bright colors with a dark one.

14

Ice-cream shades are the ultimate pastel colors.

Stick to just two pastels in one outfit to avoid sweetness overload.

Jelly shoes started as a trend in the 1980s and they are still fashionable now.

Color clash

Go wild with color-clash shorts, then balance with a solid-colored top.

Tank top

Sweatshirt

Ice-cream pastels

pastels

Pastels are milky and washed out, like ice-cream or a fuzzy dream. Wear pinks, yellows, and baby blue for a soothing set of hues.

crazy color

If you want to jump out of the box a bit, go crazy with an explosion of color! Ice-dyed pieces (see pages 16–17) are a great way to achieve this look.

ICE-DYED TOP

Fabric dyeing is like watching magic happen before your eyes! There are many different types of fabric dyeing, such as batik or tie-dye. Ice dyeing is an easy way to create shapes on fabric.

Essentials

- ☆ Cotton top
- ☆ Dish rack
- ☆ Tray or pan
- ☆ Ice cubes
- ☆ Plastic gloves
- ☆ Spoons
- ☆ Powdered fabric dye

The powdered dye sinks into the top as the ice melts.

1 **Wet your top and scrunch it up**
Place your top on the rack inside the tray. Cover it with lots of ice. Put on plastic gloves and use a spoon to sprinkle dye on the ice. The more you use, the stronger the colors will be.

Use spoons to carefully sprinkle colors onto the ice.

2 Leave the ice to melt

Leave your top for 6–8 hours until the ice is completely melted. Put on plastic gloves before taking the top out of the tray. Using cold water, rinse the top in the sink until the water is clear.

Be careful when pouring away the melted ice.

Top tip

Make sure the dye and the fabric you use work together. If your top is 100 percent cotton, use a dye for natural fabrics. Synthetic (man-made) fabrics need special dyes.

3 Your new ice-dyed top

Wash your top in the washing machine (on its own). Let it dry and enjoy your new top! Next time, mix the powdered dyes together before sprinkling them on the top and see what colors you can create.

The finished result!

If you love the watercolor-style patterns, make one for your best friend.

If you live in a cold area, you can use snow for this project!

17

Style
SEEKER

True style is as much about what you do as how you look. Maybe working in the garden gives you ideas for floral patterns or using recycled stuff helps you think of cool, quirky fashion pieces that tell a story. Design an outfit for every activity!

chilling

Try this comfortable look while hanging out with friends or just taking a relaxing walk outside.

Find tough textures for a grungy look.

Soft materials will add comfort.

Bright, happy colors boost confidence.

performing

This could be the perfect style for you if you love to perform, model, dance, or go to shows and musicals.

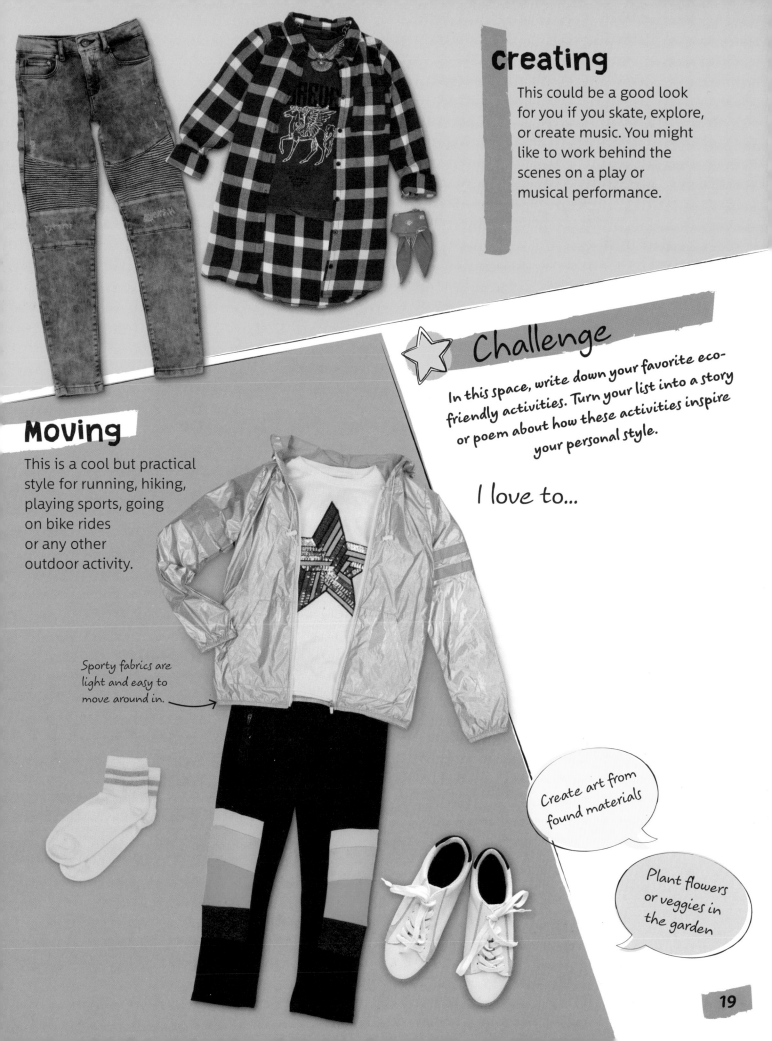

creating

This could be a good look for you if you skate, explore, or create music. You might like to work behind the scenes on a play or musical performance.

Challenge

In this space, write down your favorite eco-friendly activities. Turn your list into a story or poem about how these activities inspire your personal style.

I love to...

Moving

This is a cool but practical style for running, hiking, playing sports, going on bike rides or any other outdoor activity.

Sporty fabrics are light and easy to move around in.

Create art from found materials

Plant flowers or veggies in the garden

Create your own pattern with paper shapes. Cut out lots of shapes and glue them down. Photocopy onto transfer paper to add your pattern to a T-shirt.

Can you create a print in your sketchbook using this palette of colors?

Fuchsia

Burnt orange

Aquamarine

Designing PATTERNS

Fashion designers often work with patterns, also called prints. Designing patterns is a whole job in itself. You have to know all about color and use creativity. Use patterns in your designs for an easy way to create an instant impact.

Plaid is a traditional pattern that is also used in 90s-style grunge fashion.

Plaid

Novelty prints will get people talking.

Fruity

Checkered

Gingham is a type of **check** made from two sets of stripes.

This type of **floral** fabric is called toile. Toile means "cloth" in French.

Striped

Floral

20

the Look

This outfit is for someone who is bold and not afraid to mix and match their prints. You are a free thinker who loves to express yourself. Similar colors help to balance clashing patterns.

Raspberry pink

Teal

Stay warm with a **checkered** overcoat in a classic cocoon shape.

Rotating the pattern on the pockets makes them stand out.

Wrap up with a printed **plaid** scarf.

A cube bag hangs on the hip for a relaxed style.

Floral-patterned pants make a bold statement.

Top tip

You don't have to go for pattern overload. Try adding a checkerboard patch to your pants, wearing a pair of striped tights, popping on a polka-dot beanie, or covering up with a floral jacket.

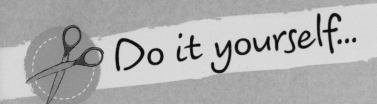

PRINT YOUR OWN PATTERN

Stamping a pattern onto fabric lets you create a cool print while showing off your artistic side. Buy premade rubber stamps at a craft store or use everyday objects from around the home to make your own stamps.

2 Design your pattern
Test your print by creating a pattern on paper. Press the stamp firmly into the ink or paint so it is covered completely, then press onto the paper. Take time to figure out which shapes you like the most.

Test out different color combinations.

Sponge shapes

1 Make a stamp
There are plenty of household objects that get the stamp of approval. Sponge or paper can be cut into any shape you like or rolled up tightly to create a rose print. Or you can buy cute rubber stamps.

Rubber stamp

Create an artist's palette of different colors.

Fabric paint

3 Stamp a patterned fabric

Now stamp your design onto fabric. Make sure you are pressing firmly into the ink or paint each time you stamp. Let the ink dry. Ask an adult for help ironing the fabric, without steam, to lock in the ink.

Collected leaf

The finished result!

Use a fabric pen to add fine details to your print.

For best results with leaf printing, paint directly on the leaf and then press it onto the paper.

Leaf print

Leaves create soft, natural shapes.

Use bottle caps to print circles.

Cut up your fabric to create something cool, such as a scarf.

Rubber stamps are great for more detailed designs.

Ink pad

23

Bag shapes

Pouch

Pouches are handy for carrying necessities such as your toothbrush.

Envelope

Keep your drawings in an **envelope** bag. This color is red hot.

A pretty bag with a chain strap will hold your things while you dance the night away!

Evening bag

Tassels or fringes look great on shoulder bags. Try one in jet black or icy white, or pair with embroidered details.

Be bold with a fruity statement bag. Pineapple is a fashion favorite.

Fun shapes

Reflect your style with a shiny shell bag.

IN the BAG

Bags come in many sizes, from tiny to extra large. Which one you choose depends on what you need to carry around. Imagine you're taking a vacation and think about what bags you'd need on your trip.

Fashion designers usually have a large bag to carry their designs and tools in.

Satchel

Buckle

The **strap** of a satchel can be worn across the body or over the shoulder.

Embroidered straw bags are a laidback choice for summer.

Handbag

The Look

This look is for someone who loves to travel—a world explorer! Effortlessly put together, you can hit the road or soar through the skies with your trusty bag on your arm.

Contrast the color of the **strap** with the body of the bag.

A jumpsuit is a comfortable traveling outfit.

You need a large, spacious bag for long trips.

Put small but important things like your passport, earphones, or gum in an **envelope bag.**

Top tip

Did you know there are designers who focus just on bags? Think like a handbag designer and draw the inside of the bag as well as the outside. Include a pocket, a patterned lining, and a label.

OUTLINES

An outline is the shape that an outfit creates when it's worn. Outlines are also called silhouettes. Adding volume to the top or bottom of an outfit creates a new outline. Legendary fashion designer Coco Chanel believed that clothes should follow the line of a person's body. Check out these outlines to see if you agree.

change the shape

Belting your outfit can change the shape of your look in a major way. From oversized sweaters to a simple dress, you can use a belt to create a totally different outline.

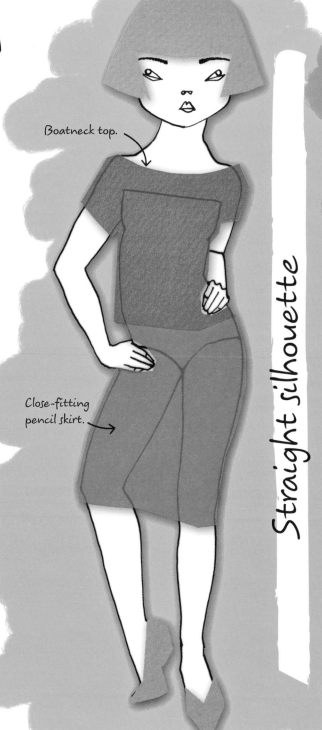

Boatneck top.

Close-fitting pencil skirt.

Straight silhouette

Basic shift dress

Pulled in with belt

Balanced

Balanced fashion looks use a straight silhouette. This gives a basic outline that is relaxed and casual, although the look can be bold, depending on the color and texture of the fabric used. This outline was popular in the 2010s.

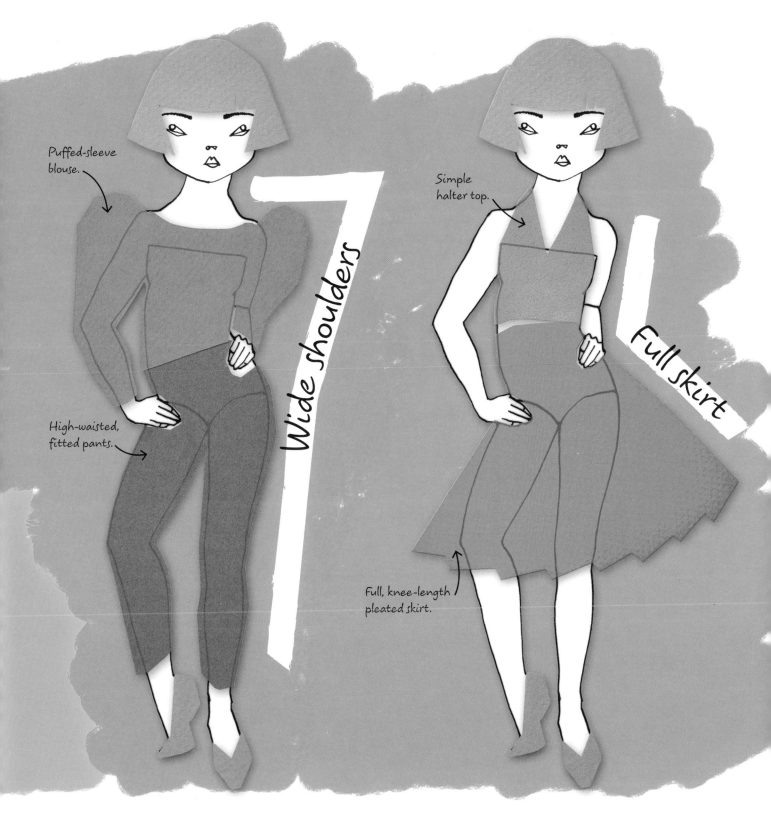

Puffed-sleeve blouse.

Wide shoulders

High-waisted, fitted pants.

Simple halter top.

Full skirt

Full, knee-length pleated skirt.

Top volume

For a dramatic, yet cool look, add volume to your top with big, puffed sleeves. This look is a modern twist on vintage clothes with shoulder pads. Top-heavy outlines were popular in the 1980s and '90s.

Fuller below

The skirt gets all the volume in this silhouette. Puffy and pleated skirts made from tulle, cotton, or other swishy fabrics are fab and fun to twirl in. This outline was popular in the 1950s and early '60s.

Balloons

Bright yellow

Sky blue

Juicy orange

Use bright balloon colors in a design. What fabrics mimic their texture?

Bunting adds movement and color to the party space.

Create a party outfit using this outrageous celebration palette.

READY to PARTY!

Parties are a ball! We get to show off our sparkling side and have fun. Each season brings reasons to celebrate, for instance, your birthday or the end of the school year. So, twirl around and dance while you plan what you'll wear. Where will this amazing party outfit take you?

Try pastels for a sweet twist on bright colors.

Birthday cake

Use sequins that look like cake sprinkles on your designs.

Cake pops

Find the contrasting colors in these candies and use them to design a palette.

Use the eye-catching colors of presents as inspiration, then top your design with a **bow**.

The Look

Stand out at the party in a fierce and unforgettable outfit. This person is not afraid to go all out to be memorable. Whether the party is an artsy gathering or a glittering disco, they think like a fashion superhero.

Mint green

Hot pink

Chandelier earrings are great when you want to feel extra special.

What texture would your party outfit have? Silky fabrics create a shining surface.

This dress is decorated with a huge sky-blue and yellow **bow** for maximum impact.

Embellish the skirt with trim to look like a layered **birthday cake**.

Bright blocks of **candy-colored** fabric are perfect for a celebration.

29

Love your DENIM

Denim is the best fabric to DIY because it's sturdy, making it easy to cut and embellish just the way you like. Design a denim jacket that matches your style or challenge yourself to try a totally new denim accessory!

Light or dark?

Denim is described as being a light or dark wash. Try on both to see which you prefer.

Light denim

Dark denim

Embellishments show up better on light wash.

One jacket, three ways

In your sketchbook, write at least three steps that you will take to complete a jacket redesign. This is your process. Successful fashion designers always have a process, so it's good for you to have one, too.

Add patches

Play around with where you place your patches. Go with the ideas that pop out at you!

Some patches can be ironed on, or you can sew or safety pin them on.

Dark wash is classic and goes with everything.

Denim all over

Denim is always popular because it truly fits any style. Here are a few items you might wear with your awesome upcycled jacket.

Overalls

After cutting, you can fray away (see page 33) to create a textured edge.

snip the sleeves

If the sleeves on your jacket are not working for you, give them a snip (but ask permission first). A denim vest looks stylish over long-sleeved tops.

!

If you decide to sew by hand, use a tiny running stitch (see page 7).

!

Decorate the back

Cover the back of your jacket with a piece of fabric by cutting it to fit. Then machine or hand-sew it on.

Stitch on a few tassels to make your jacket extra fancy.

Bag

Try adding some patches to a light denim backpack.

Skirt

Frayed shoe bows give an edge to your denim outfit.

Shoes

Denim caps are great for adding a pop of denim to an outfit.

Hat

DESIGNER DENIM

Let's take a moment to think about the possibilities of denim. Denim is a strong cotton fabric that is usually blue. It can be used for all sorts of clothing, such as overalls, skirts, and (you guessed it) jeans! Grab the materials that you'll need and get creative.

Essentials

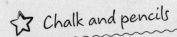

- ☆ Chalk and pencils
- ☆ Jeans
- ☆ Scissors
- ☆ Patterned material
- ☆ Needle and thread
- ☆ Fabric paint
- ☆ Pom-pom trim

1 Mark your design
Use chalk or a pencil to draw the shapes that you want on your jeans. Try on the jeans before you cut them to make sure the shapes are in the right places.

2 Add fabric
Cut out a fabric shape just a bit bigger than the hole you've made. Turn the jeans inside out, then sew on the shape using a running stitch (see page 7) so it covers the hole.

3 Outline with paint
Using fabric paint or a fabric pen, carefully draw around the shapes you have cut to outline them.

Shiny or colorful fabrics look great with denim.

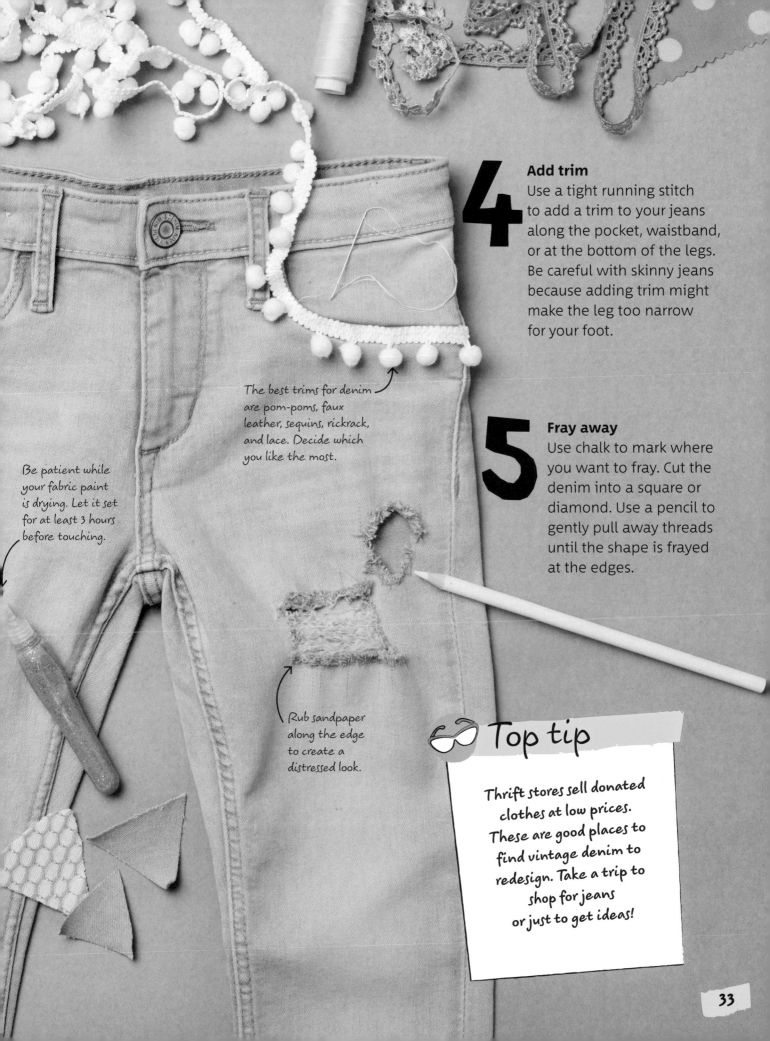

4 Add trim

Use a tight running stitch to add a trim to your jeans along the pocket, waistband, or at the bottom of the legs. Be careful with skinny jeans because adding trim might make the leg too narrow for your foot.

5 Fray away

Use chalk to mark where you want to fray. Cut the denim into a square or diamond. Use a pencil to gently pull away threads until the shape is frayed at the edges.

The best trims for denim are pom-poms, faux leather, sequins, rickrack, and lace. Decide which you like the most.

Be patient while your fabric paint is drying. Let it set for at least 3 hours before touching.

Rub sandpaper along the edge to create a distressed look.

Top tip

Thrift stores sell donated clothes at low prices. These are good places to find vintage denim to redesign. Take a trip to shop for jeans or just to get ideas!

Types of shoe

Wedge sandal

Go for solids or small polka dots when choosing your summer sandal "solemate."

Sneaker

The athletic craze started in the '80s. Sneakers are now an everyday part of fashion.

Lace-up boot

These boots have comfortable **rubber soles**. You can wear them with almost anything.

Rain boot

Rain boots were originally made of leather but are now made from rubber. Much dryer!

Ballet flats

Easy to fit and to slip on, flats are stars among shoes.

Mary Janes

Mary Janes have a strap to keep your feet secure.

Loafers

You can wear a loose dress with a pair of loafers for a free-spirited look.

WALK with STYLE

Looking down at comfortable, cute shoes brings great joy. It's like your feet are smiling back at you! Click your heels together and get to know these different types of shoes. Pair yourself with the shoe shape that suits your style and helps you explore the world around you.

Socks with sandals can be a strong fashion look. Try patterned knee-high socks with sandals in the fall and spring.

Roller skates come in all colors and patterns to match your look. Be safe and have fun rolling on by.

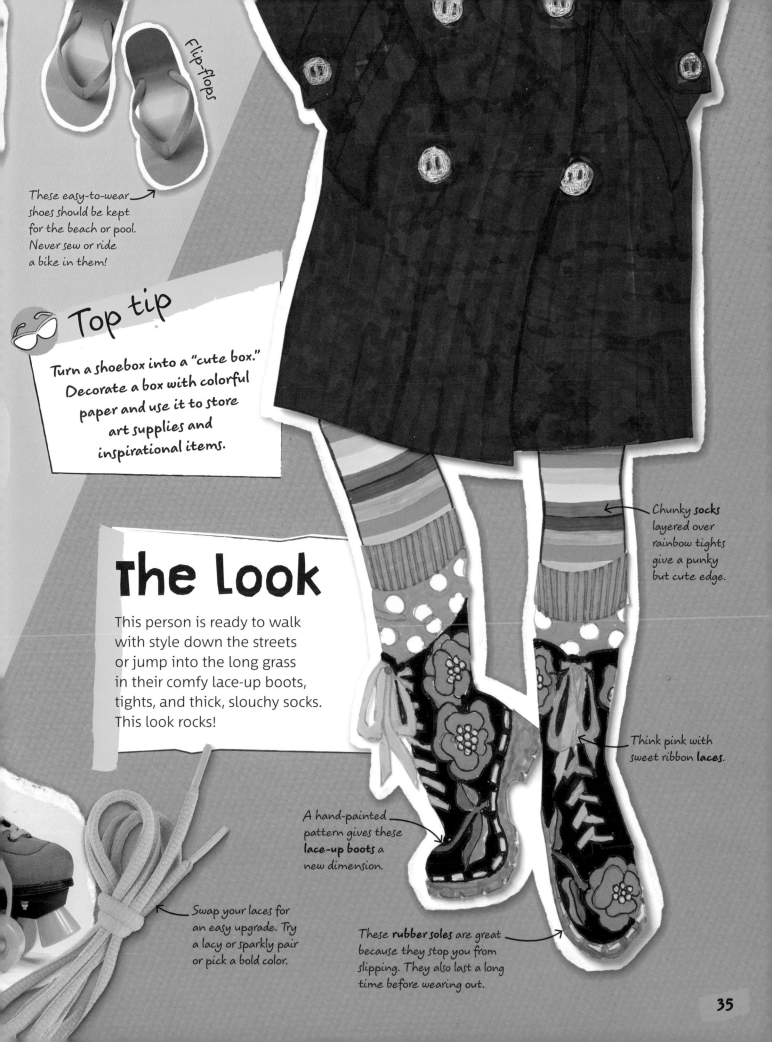

Flip-flops

These easy-to-wear shoes should be kept for the beach or pool. Never sew or ride a bike in them!

Top tip

Turn a shoebox into a "cute box." Decorate a box with colorful paper and use it to store art supplies and inspirational items.

The Look

This person is ready to walk with style down the streets or jump into the long grass in their comfy lace-up boots, tights, and thick, slouchy socks. This look rocks!

Chunky **socks** layered over rainbow tights give a punky but cute edge.

Think pink with sweet ribbon **laces**.

A hand-painted pattern gives these **lace-up boots** a new dimension.

Swap your laces for an easy upgrade. Try a lacy or sparkly pair or pick a bold color.

These **rubber soles** are great because they stop you from slipping. They also last a long time before wearing out.

Bring your camera or phone. Take photos of the sights you find interesting and add your fave images to your mood board.

Sea green

Ocean blue

Red

Look at all the bright colors around you at the beach and use them in your designs.

Use your sketchbook while you're at the beach to draw **wave** shapes.

Rope can be used for bags, a bracelet, or other accessories.

At the
BEACH

Going to the beach is an adventure for your senses! The wind on your skin, salt in the air, and stunning views can all inspire you to design and create a whole beach look of your own.

Rope

Collect pebbles

The vibrant color of **coral** brightens any ensemble.

Striped shells

Coral

Sandy yellow

See the patterns in **ice-cream** swirls and a waffle cone.

A shell and bead tiara crowns this girl's flaming hair.

A parasol protects the girl's skin and is the turquoise of a tropical sea.

The Look

This ocean-inspired look includes the colors and shapes of the sea, as well as things you might find at the beach. Add an amazing shell tiara to keep the look high-fashion.

A gorgeous **coral**-colored plastic necklace adds a color pop.

This top is in light, breezy cotton.

A bracelet made from **rope**.

Be a rock star! Use the color and feel of pebbles for inspiration.

The ruffle reflects the flowing shapes of ocean **waves**.

Challenge

Plan out your beach look— match the colors and patterns of your swimsuit, towel, bag, and hat and bring a piece of matching fabric to lie on while you rest and read.

The pink laces were inspired by raspberry-ripple **ice cream**.

Do it yourself...

STYLISH SHOES

Essentials

☆ White shoes

☆ Paint pens (or fabric pens)

☆ Ribbon

You don't have to spend a lot on a pair of shiny new shoes! Picking the perfect pair can say a lot about your personality, while at the same time tying your whole look together. Grab your supplies and get ready to craft. All eyes will be on you—or at least on your customized sneakers.

1 Plan your project
Choose a pair of plain shoes to decorate. In your sketchbook, practice your design. Make notes of all the details, such as shapes, colors, and embellishments.

Ribbon

Plain white shoes work best for this project.

White shoes

Paint pens

38

Let your paints dry before you add any other details so that your design doesn't smudge. You can add more layers and features to your design once the color underneath is dry!

Try to match the color of the paint across different sections.

Think about what colors might work well together or that you think will match your style!

2 Draw on your shoes

Use paint pens (or fabric pens on softer material) to draw your favorite patterns. Try color-blocking with bright shades.

3 Add ribbon laces

Embellish your shoes by replacing your laces with colored ribbon. Make sure you lace up both of your shoes the same way!

Metallic ribbon colors will work well here.

Wow!

The finished result!

39

Hat shapes

Wool hat with earflaps

A knitted cap brings texture to a winter look.

Porkpie

A porkpie hat has a small brim and a dent in the crown (top).

Ears

Hats can be playful! This **straw** hat with ears is the cat's meow.

Beanie

Head-hugging and brimless, beanies are really comfy.

Floppy hat

Wear a big floppy hat to be noticed, but also to stay mysterious under the brim.

Beret

A beret is usually made from wool. It's soft and cozy in cold weather.

Baseball cap

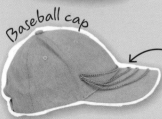

Baseball caps are fun to embellish. Get a plain one and add flowers, chains, or a string of pearls.

HEAD in the CLOUDS

It's okay to have your head in the clouds when you're wearing a hat. If you are a hat person, here are a few shapes to try and work into your style. Crown your look with the headgear that suits you best.

Top off your look with a tiara. A tiara is a crown with jewels, such as rhinestones.

A summer hat with tassels is perfect for the beach, a summer market, or a street fair.

The Look

This person likes to keep their cool and is always creating a style of their own. A hat and scarf combo is the perfect way to top off a simple outfit. The ribbon and blossoms make the fedora pop, while the patterned scarf frames the face.

Adorn your head with a band full of **blossoms**.

Decorate the hat with a ribbon band and **blossom**.

The wide brim of the **straw** hat will give shade from the sun.

The bold, bright pattern on this **headscarf** makes the look fashionable and fun.

To make a **headscarf**, fold fabric in a triangle shape, put it on your head with the fold at the back, and tie a knot at the front.

A T-shirt keeps the style casual by balancing out the fabulous headgear.

Jackets

Add an embroidered patch or appliqué to create original outerwear.

Denim

Blazer

Parka

Dresses and skirts

Dresses are great because you can easily dress them up or down. How about layering one over jeans?

Skater

Skirt

Striped

SHOP your CLOSET

Before you spend your precious money buying more clothes, shop your closet! Give items a longer life by taking good care of them, and create new looks by mixing things you've never worn together before. See how it's done with this colorful cardigan.

 ## Clothing care

☆ Spot-clean splatters: gently blot away any spills on clothes with a damp cloth right away, so they don't set in.

☆ Flip it inside out: turning clothes inside out before washing protects the colors and any decorations like prints, appliqué, or sequins.

☆ Hang or fold right away: as soon as clothes are dry, hang them up or fold them neatly to prevent wrinkles.

weekday chic

It may just be a normal school day, but you can create a chic and sporty outfit no matter the event.

Don't cover it up—let the colors shine!

Decorate your own shoes for customization.

Jeans

Leggings

Pants

Pants

Hunt until you find the perfect pants. They should be the ideal length to show off your shoes.

Tops

Shirts are super fun to style. Layer sleeveless tops over dresses and shirts.

Sleeveless

Graphic tee

Button-down

Accessories

Accessories add fun to your outfit. Notice the compliments you get when you wear them.

Headband

Hat

Backpack

Socks

Love your accessories? Read pages 40–41 for inspiration on fun headwear.

Contrasting with darker shoes always works well.

Day out

You are a person on the go! On Saturdays and school breaks, pull out the special items you rarely wear.

Party time

For a school dance or a family party, pick a look that is playful but comfortable. In winter, add a warm jacket.

Jackets can be chic as well as practical.

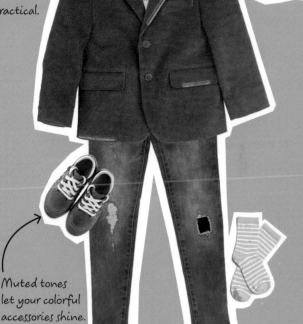

Muted tones let your colorful accessories shine.

Cardigan

Sweater

Hoodie

sweaters and cardigans

Snuggly sweaters are the perfect layer to wear over any outfit you like.

Sneakers

Flats

Shoes

shoes

Choose shoes made from material that lets air flow to prevent blisters and smelly feet.

Fern

Tropical leaf

Create a mood board using this nature-inspired color palette!

Fuchsia

Fresh green

Mulberry

Lavender

Petal pink

Lemon yellow

Add leaves to your designs by cutting shapes out of **green** felt or by stamping them on.

Look at
NATURE

Let's take a fresh look at nature for inspiration. Use leaves, plants, and flowers to discover amazing color combinations and textures. Are you ready to go hunting for inspiration in the natural world?

Bumpy cactus

Try using the texture of a cactus, or even add spikes to your designs.

Top tip

Houseplants can be highly stylish! Get an easy-to-grow plant such as a succulent or cactus to bring nature into your room. Have fun developing "green thumbs"!

Peony

Spiked cacti

Poppy

the Look

Turn over a new leaf in this nature-filled, boho look! This outfit is for someone who loves to stroll around in gardens, or just bring some flower power to the streets of town.

Silk or plastic **flowers** make great hair accessories.

Sketch your favorite **flowers**, then work them into one of your designs.

A dark background on a pretty floral print top makes the look edgier.

Try a **leaf**-shaped belt buckle.

A strong **green** color shows off these simple, cropped pants.

This tote bag has a cute **cactus** and heart appliqué.

Flowers are powerful as well as pretty — they grow from tiny seeds into beautiful blooms.

Wooden clogs keep to the natural theme.

45

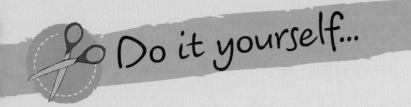
PANDA PATCH

An appliqué is a small piece of fabric sewn onto a larger piece to create a design. Adding an appliqué is a method that fashion designers use to make a basic garment stand out. Create an appliqué for your T-shirt!

1 Draw your favorite animal

Once you've decided on a cool animal, draw it to the size you want your appliqué to be. Carefully cut out the shapes to create a template for your design.

2 Cut out felt shapes

Trace around the paper template to mark the animal's face onto your fabric. Use small fabric scissors to cut it out.

Ears

Face

Nose

Mouth

Don't forget smaller shapes for the little details.

3

Glue the patch together
Use fabric glue to stick the face together. Let it dry for at least one hour. Use a fabric marker to add detail to your animal's face.

Top tip

Use paint to create an environment for your animal. Place a piece of cardboard on the inside of the shirt to stop the paint from soaking through, then paint on trees or leaves. Pandas prefer bamboo forests.

Use green paint to draw leaves and plants.

The finished result!

Challenge

You can use the appliqué process to make a cat, fox, or maybe a jellyfish. You can even add animal paw prints or zebra stripes to your clothes!

4

Sew on your patch
After the glue is dry on your appliqué, pin it to the T-shirt using dressmaker's pins—ask an adult for help with this. Then use a running stitch (see page 7) to sew it on.

PIECE TOGETHER
– your –
STYLE!

Just like putting together a puzzle, building a style is about fitting different pieces together to show who you are. Each item you choose to wear is a piece of your fashion puzzle. So, let's put them all together! Remember, every icon starts somewhere.

Tip 1: color your world
Mix and match bold colors as if you're grouping together pieces that might match in a certain part of a puzzle. Why not try a sunny yellow top with ocean-blue jeans or a green hoodie with purple pants? Bold color options can make every day feel like an artsy party!

Tip 2: accessory adventures
Hunt for cool accessories like hats, scarves, earrings, sunglasses, and fancy socks. They're like the missing puzzle piece that can turn a plain outfit into an artistic look for any occasion.

Tip 3: pattern play
Stripes, florals, polka dots, plaids—you **can** choose more than one! Wear different patterns together to highlight your style. It's an interesting part of your puzzle that you get to put together. Fun!

Tip 4: upcycle = unique
Find old clothes and add your own twist using patches or paint. It's a blast to turn something old into a brand-new item. Upcycled items could be the edge pieces of your puzzle, forming the basic outline.

Tip 5: complete the puzzle
Step back and look in a full-length mirror. Does your look feel like you or the person you want to become? If not, swap pieces until you see the complete picture of your style. Don't forget your smile!

Harry plays with unconventional patterns and a relaxed silhouette. It's a mix-and-match of playful textures and vintage vibes, creating a unique and eclectic fashion statement that puts him outside of the box.

Harry's puzzle...

Vintage vibes

Harry Styles

Bold colors

Janelle Monáe

Janelle's puzzle...

Janelle's puzzle is all about strong, tailored lines and a powerful color palette. Her look is classic with a twist—sharp suits in vibrant hues accented with delicate details, both sophisticated and daring.

My puzzle is...

Both singers' puzzles are completed with personal touches that make their outfits distinctly theirs and tell us something about their personality. Style is about self-expression. What will you express with yours?

49

TEXTURE

Texture is about the look and feel of materials. Fashion designers add texture to their creations by using a mixture of fabrics and trims. The next time you're looking at fabrics, think about how they feel: which ones are smooth, rough, fuzzy, gritty, or even slippery?

Tough

Tough fabrics are usually heavy and strong. For example, denim was originally worn by men working in construction because it was hard to rip. Tough fabrics are tightly woven, with hundreds of little threads.

Leather is strong and comfortable, but expensive.

Leather

Denim is always popular because it is smooth and strong.

Denim

scratchy

Scratchy fabrics are often lined with softer fabrics to protect our skin. In some cases, scratchy materials lose their stiffness when they are washed.

Lace

Tulle

Sequined

Sequins are tiny, flat disks made from plastic.

smooth

Smooth, slippery fabrics make beautiful clothes that are often soft and light. Silk and velvet are perfect for evening gowns.

⭐ Challenge

Go to your closet and find at least three textures. Put them together to create an outfit that you've never tried before.

Linen

Silk

Velvet

Cotton

Wool

Fake fur

Velvet is smooth because of its pile. The pile is like lots of hairs on the fabric's surface.

Fleece

Light

Light fabrics are thin. These materials are perfect for the summer months because they won't make you sweat.

warm and fuzzy

Fabrics that are warm and fuzzy are often used to keep us cozy in the cooler months. These fabrics have the most texture of all because they are made up of chunky fibers woven together.

51

FEEL the fun

Every fabric has a story. Touch it, wear it, and play with it! Mixing textures is like mixing paint—it's all about creating something that's new and uniquely you. So, next time you get dressed, get tactile with different pieces, and let your fashion sense "feel" the fun—what a mood booster!

Layer it on

Start with a simple, basic outfit, then add layers of texture. Layered textures look interesting and feel even better. And feeling good leads to looking good!

Fluffy

Crinkly

Try out textures

People who work in fashion call the feel of fabric against your skin the "hand" of a fabric. The next time you are in a store or looking in your closet, touch different textures. What is the "hand" of the fabric? Is it soft, rough, crinkly, fluffy, or smooth?

My favorite textures

What textures do you like best? Write them here or in your sketchbook. Next time you are at a fabric store, ask for samples of these materials to add to your mood board.

Patterns

Polka dots

Houndstooth

There are so many black-and-white **patterns**—it's fun to mix them up!

Use iron-on photo transfer paper to put a black-and-white photo onto a T-shirt.

Waves

Silhouettes

Curvy

BLACK and WHITE

Designing with black and white is timeless, meaning that it never goes out of style. Fashion designers love working with this color combination and create all sorts of designs, from peaceful to punchy. Here is some inspiration to get you started.

Show your wild side and take inspiration from zebra **stripes**.

Zebra

Use black-and-white fake fur to give a **panda** vibe to your look.

Add different-shaped buttons in black and white to your clothes.

Panda

Dalmatian spots are as neat as polka dots. Consider using them in your next design.

Dalmatian

The Look

This person keeps it casual and chic with a streetwear look inspired by black-and-white animals. From snow-white to jet-black, fashion magic happens when these opposites attract.

Striped sweaters make a classic statement.

Stack chunky black and white bangles.

Add a **panda** patch or keyring to the bag.

Layer a crisp white shirt under a shorter sweater.

Get a sporty look with striped joggers.

Checkered slip-ons pack in an extra **pattern**.

Top tip

When designing with black and white, if you wear a loud top or bottom, keep the other clothes simple. For example, wear a plain black or white top with loud zebra-print leggings.

Fashion REMIX

Styling with black and white is easy because you can't go wrong. You will always match when you combine black and white no matter what patterns or textures you add. Use your imagination when mixing and matching with black and white to create new looks.

SWAP IT!

Patterned

Carry a simple, chic white backpack with black details.

For a fun pop of pattern, swap a plain backpack for a polka-dot black-and-white one.

Black and white is a classic color combination for sneakers.

Dash of color

Shoes are a great way to add a splash of color to your black-and-white outfit.

The same design can look completely different in black or white. A white lace top looks pretty and bohemian, while the same top in black looks more glamorous and gothic.

A (faux) leather jacket is a great way to add a cool edge to your ensemble.

For a pretty, daytime look, pair a white top with jeans.

Layered

The black version of this top is great if you like an edgy, cool style.

Try a nautical look with a simple, striped T-shirt.

Create a fun, layered look by swapping your T-shirt for a short, pleated dress.

White jeans look crisp and fresh. Don't wear them anywhere muddy though!

⭐ Challenge

Try black-and-white dressing for one week. Create looks by mixing prints and solids, going monochrome (one color) and color-blocking. Note down which are your best outfits and why.

Statement

If white jeans aren't for you, replace them with a statement pair of joggers.

Get in the zone by listening to music on headphones while you are designing.

Headphones

Bright yellow

Use these colors to create a performance-themed mood board.

Lime green

Flame red

Cool blue

Zesty orange

Speaker

Turn up the MUSIC

What would soundwaves look like if you could see them?

If you are into fashion, you probably love music too! There is a close relationship between fashion and music. Fashion designers need music for their shows and parties, while performers need clothes that will look great on stage. Let music help you develop a rocking look.

Electric guitar

Concert

Electric **guitars** come in all kinds of designs, from sunrise orange to traditional wood.

Join the fan club and be inspired by band T-shirts from concerts and festivals. A concert T looks amazing with denim.

the Look

This outfit is loud and upbeat, with a fast tempo! The laid-back T-shirt and jeans, combined with lightning-bolt earrings, scream "I'm ready to dance." You'll want to replay this look more than once.

Mirror ball

⭐ Challenge

Listen to at least five different types of music, such as jazz, grunge, rock, pop, and hip-hop. Then create an outfit inspired by the music you like best.

Keep your **headphones** handy so you can listen to your favorite playlist.

The silver **guitar** T-shirt is inspired by watching a favorite band live.

A silver chain bracelet will shine like a **mirror ball**.

Decorate your designing space with cute musical tech, such as mini speakers.

This bag was inspired by old-school vinyl records.

Flared disco jeans embroidered with rainbow confetti shapes are perfect for dancing.

Sneakers with studded toes bring in a rocky edge.

UPCYCLING

Have you ever heard of upcycling? It's like a game you can play with your own wardrobe, someone else's, or with thrift-store finds. With upcycling, old clothes get to go on an adventure to become something totally new! It is an opportunity for you to refresh an item that was already loved by giving it a second life.

Wardrobes are like time capsules! Trends very often come back around.

What's Upcycling?

Upcycling is the process of taking clothes that are tired, out-of-style, or just plain "blah," and turning them into fab new pieces that are fresh and fun. Use what you already own to make fashion magic!

Upcycling isn't new—it's a technique that's been around for a while. But guess what? Now there are designers and entire stores that specialize in turning discarded clothes into trendy, must-have pieces. These places are like playgrounds for your imagination, packed with inspiration. Go window shopping for ideas and see what you discover.

Thrift shopping can be a fun day out with friends!

say "no thanks" to fast fashion

What's fast fashion? Fast fashion is essentially clothing that is made superfast in a factory and that doesn't stick around for long. We're not fans of fast fashion, because it's not kind to our planet—many of the pieces are poorly made from materials that can be harmful to the environment. When we upcycle and thrift shop, we're saying "We love the Earth and we want a positive future for the planet"—in the most stylish way possible!

Upcycling is different from recycling. It transforms an object without first breaking it down.

Pre-loved fashion is kind to the planet.

Draw your cutting guide to match this.

1 Mark your cutting outline

Draw out the "handles" of your bag on your T-shirt. Cut off the sleeves and make a deeper cut into the neckline. Repeat this on the back.

A T-shirt's life cycle

Imagine a T-shirt's journey: from a cozy fit you loved, to a bit too tight, to becoming an awesome art project! Add paint, cut it into a totally new shape, or dye it a funky color. That's upcycling—giving items endless lives so they can be loved over and over again! There are so many possibilities.

2 Transform your T

Turn your T-shirt inside out. Sew the bottom edges together with a running stitch. Flip it back out and you have a bag!

A brand new bag!

sparkle it up

Try a full-shimmer look with clothes, shoes, and accessories— you can even put gems in your hair accessories. Pile on the shimmer and sparkle, then work backward to see if there's anything you want to take off.

A sequined dress always creates a red-carpet moment.

Buy or borrow a stack of bangles. They'll make you feel festive.

Throw all your stuff into a glittery bag and you're ready to go.

Sparkle socks will make your outfit rock.

Be the star that you are in metallic shoes! You can dress them up or down.

GLITZ and GLAM

If you want to shimmer and sparkle, let's create a casual or dressed-up look that will fit your style. Turn everywhere you go into your catwalk!

A touch of sparkle

If you're not into extreme sparkle, try a T-shirt embellished with jewels or sequins. Throw on a pair of jeans and let the fun begin!

Sequin patches and embellishment give a casual touch of sparkle.

Keep your accessories cute with fun shapes.

Sequins in the same color as your outfit will shine in a subtle way.

Walk like a star in glittery shoes.

Top tip

Make sure you approve of your sparkly look by using a full-length mirror before going out. What are your eyes drawn to? Remember to finish the look with a sparkling smile!

Finish the Look

There are many ways to add glitz and glam to your look. Don't be afraid to dazzle. It's way more fun to look like a movie star than it is to look at one!

Face sparkle!

On your face, experiment with stick-on jewels (or eyelash glue). You can also glue jewels onto your hair accessories for added shine.

Gold is measured in karats. Pure gold is 24 karats.

Gold

Silver charm bracelet

Silver

Garnet

Ruby

Diamond

Amethyst

Pearl

Adding charms to a bracelet is a good way to celebrate milestones in your life.

Heart pendant

Sapphire

Opal

Bring on the bling with a statement ring.

Flower ring

Joyful
JEWELRY

Jewelry is both pretty and powerful. Throughout history it has been used for good luck and protection. Wear favorite pieces when you want to calm yourself before a test or you need a burst of confidence.

Gold chain

Hang your **necklaces** and chains up when you're not wearing them so they don't get tangled.

Owl brooch

Brooches are like art you can wear. Pin one on your top, sweater, coat, or even your hat.

Earrings come in many styles, from studs to chandeliers. This pair is for pierced ears, but you can also buy clip-ons.

Buy or make your own beaded necklace. Layer different textures and lengths, then showcase them by wearing with a simple T-shirt.

Beaded necklace

Emerald

Peridot

Aquamarine

Topaz

Turquoise

Pick your favorite gem and make it your signature jewel.

the Look

Let your confidence shine through with a set of jewels that reflects your personality. Adorn yourself with a few favorites or sprinkle on a lot of bling. The only rule is to be yourself!

Think outside the box and design a piece of jewelry for your head or feet.

Get a pair of matching friendship bracelets. Give one to a friend to be bracelet buddies.

This signature **earring** shape is a heart. Stars, half-moons, and ice-cream cones are also great shapes.

This statement **necklace** fits an outrageous style. A simple top balances the look.

A **pendant** can be any shape or size, such as this huge, colorful bird!

65

Beaded necklace

Royal blue

Golden yellow

Use these regal colors to create your Egyptian-inspired look.

Deep red

Turquoise

The Egyptians **pleated** cloth to create dramatic clothing.

Queen Nefertiti was adored for her beauty. She ruled with her husband around 1300 BCE.

Queen Nefertiti

Dress like an
ANCIENT
EGYPTIAN

The ancient Egyptians are known for their rich history, attention to detail, and magnificent style. Combine historic items to create an Egyptian-inspired look. Are you ready to explore the beauty in ancient Egyptian fashion? Let's travel back in time!

Bracelet

Scarab beetles were the ancient Egyptians' favorite bugs!

This sculpture of King Tut is made of real gold and precious gems.

Scarab beetle brooch

Sacred eye

Tutankhamun

The Look

This outfit features a softly pleated dress, detailed bomber jacket, and amazing jewelry. Gold was very popular in ancient Egypt. When you create your look, be sure to wear golden, copper, or bronze pieces.

Wrap a scarf around your head for elegant **Queen Nefertiti** style.

Adorn yourself with accessories such as gemstone earrings, rings, and bracelets.

The **scarab beetle** inspired this embellishment on a silky bomber jacket.

Regal purple

Challenge

Plan an Egyptian-themed treasure swap with your friends. Ask everyone to bring a special item to swap. Think gold-colored charms, royal-blue nail polish, or gemstone rings!

Golden snake cuff

Channel the regal gowns of the Egyptians with a **pleated** dress.

Keep the look relaxed with knotted slides — or go barefoot.

WRAP up WARM

From capelike sweaters to star-filled rain jackets, your goal in the fall and winter is to stay warm and dry. Use these looks for inspiration, then create a style storm by wrapping up in your own way.

Some days are too cold to be fall, but too warm to be winter. These are the perfect times for layering. Try on a cape or a thin scarf to keep breezes at bay.

Be the star that you are in a patterned raincoat.

A knitted cape will show off your style in a textured way.

Fall showers

When the cold rain drizzles down, slip into your rain boots, grab your umbrella, and pull on a fun printed coat.

Find patterned over-the-knee socks or tights that fit your style.

Corduroy is snug when it's breezy outside.

Rain boots come in the coolest prints.

Grab a circle scarf to make your look well-rounded.

Fuzzy hats are wonderful and warm. Double pom-poms help you stand out in the crowd.

⭐ Challenge

Light up the fall in lighter colors, such as cream, beige, and ocher (a warm, spicy yellow). Who says you can't look bright even when it's dark outside? You can design dramatic coats in all sorts of colors and patterns.

Winter weather

Get the best outerwear by spending plenty of time trying on coats before choosing one. It's worth it, since you'll wear a coat every day when the skies are gray.

Get a lightweight, yet warm, quilted puffer jacket in a color you adore.

Be dressy but comfortable in a pair of leather slide-on boots.

Cuffed legs keep cold winds out.

Shearling (sheepskin) boots are the best for cozy toes!

YOUR CREATIVE JOURNEY

Fashion designers create look books to tell a story through their designs. Are you ready to capture and document your creative process? It's a way to showcase your style and your journey as a young designer. Here's how to put together a fabulous look book that could one day be your very own designer portfolio!

How to take great photos

 Grab your shutterbug friends and plan your shoot.

 Set the mood with music.

 Find natural light whenever possible.

 Stand up straight.

 If you feel awkward close your eyes for a few seconds and think of a happy place.

 SMILE (photoshoots don't have to be super serious. Have fun!)

capture your creations!

Use your camera to take high-quality photos of your designs. Whether it's clothes you've made or upcylced, or outfits you've styled, make sure they're the star of the show. It's fine to use mobile phones to capture these photos.

Create a few fun props to use on your shoot. Try flowers, inflatables, or toys.

set the scene

Find cool spots that will make your outfits pop and will create a mood. Your bedroom, a garden, or colorful street art can be awesome backdrops. The right setting can bring your fashion story to life!

Keep an eye out for interesting textures. In the city, this could be bricks, steel, concrete, or stone.

Tell a story

For each photo, write a little note about what inspired you, the materials you used, and what makes this design special. It's your design diary, or your very own magazine!

Type out or handwrite
your design diary.
You are the editor,
so let it flow!

Share Your Vision

Once your look book is complete, share it with your friends and family. You never know who will be inspired by what you do!

"Composition" is
the way you arrange
different things
in the photo,
including yourself.

Personal Touch

Add doodles, stickers, or fabric swatches to your look-book pages. This is not just a portfolio, it's a piece of art! Include your mood board, too—maybe that becomes the cover.

Create a geometric
background using chunky
shapes cut out of paper.

A block of color shows off cool
textures and outlines. Get a
huge sheet of poster board to
use as a backdrop.

Get cosmic inspiration from **space**. Copy the shapes and silvery glow of the moon and stars.

Taupe

Night-sky blue

Use this kaleidoscope of nighttime colors to create an out-of-this-world look.

Moon and stars

Soft blue

In your DREAMS

The nights when you get to stay up late and have fun with friends and family are magical and memorable. Check out this inspiration for super-cozy bedtime fashion. Sweet dreams!

Fairy lights

Decorate your room with fairy lights for a whimsical sleep or work space.

Sleepy polar bear

Pillow fight!

Did you know kittens spend 16–20 hours napping each day? Channel their **fuzzy** fur and relaxed vibe.

Down pillows are made from the feathers of geese and ducks.

Feathers have a mix of straight and fluffy edges.

Top tip

Use a feather or decorate a piece of cardboard with favorites from your art supplies to make your own bookmark.

Teal

Heather purple

The Look

This cozy look is perfect for a friend's sleepover or a movie night on the sofa with family. When designing your own outfit, keep fabrics soft and snuggly for ultimate sleepwear style.

The contrasting-color trim along the edge of this gown is called piping.

Upcycle sleepwear by adding an appliqué, such as this **space-inspired** astrocat (see pages 46–47).

The nightgown is the deep blue of a **night sky.**

Add big pockets for treasures or useful things, such as a pencil for writing in your journal.

Grab a good book and read in bed, or jot down your dreams in a journal when you wake up.

Think about the season when designing a robe. **Fuzzy** fleece is best for winter, while cotton is cool for summer.

Bear-faced slippers keep feet comfy and warm for midnight snack runs.

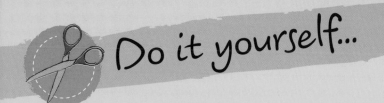

SHIRT RESCUE

You can upcycle clothes that feel a bit tired with a few tricks to improve them. You've learned the running stitch (see page 7). Now gather your sewing kit and a boring shirt you never liked and get started.

Essentials

☆ A boring shirt

☆ Needle and thread

☆ Buttons and fasteners

☆ Fabric scraps

☆ Lace trim

If you don't have matching thread, try a color contrast.

After the makeover!

This fastener is called a frog. Frogs are both useful and decorative. Ribbit!

Before

1 Rethink the sleeves
Roll up the sleeves and fix them in place with a fastener (an item that holds clothes closed). If the sleeves are too slouchy, hem them with a running stitch.

!

2

Add a lacy collar
Pin your lace around the collar to make sure it is long enough. Use a running stitch to neatly sew it on, making sure the lace is flat as you go.

This lace trim would also look cute on a T-shirt.

!

3

Sew on a pocket
Carefully cut a pocket shape out of fabric and stitch it on. Leave the edges frayed or fold them under, depending on how polished you want the shirt to look.

Leave the top of the pocket open so you can tuck away earphones or lip balm.

Sew all the way around your patch to stop the threads from unraveling.

!

4

Swap out the buttons
Replacing plain buttons is the easiest way to perk up your shirt! You can use matching buttons or mix them all up.

Challenge

What types of fastener could you add to your shirt? The ancient Indus Valley people made buttons from seashells, while modern designers use laces, safety pins, and snaps.

Design your own... T-SHIRT

A T-shirt is a blank canvas where you can add your favorite things. Try patterns or drawings based on the food, animal, or activity you love most.

Express yourself
Go wild with doodles on this plain T-shirt.

Use your favorite colors

Use words or phrases in your design.

Hey!

LOL

I love cats

Draw your favorite things

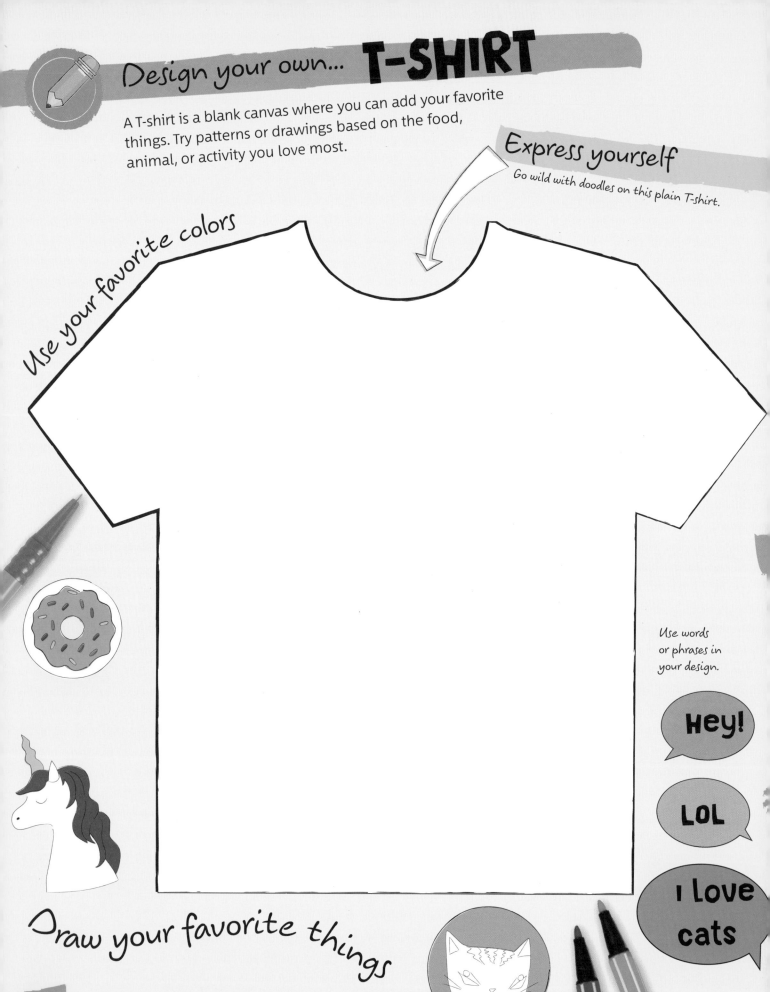

Add a pattern

Design a pattern using simple shapes and symbols.

Design your logo

Design a logo by writing your name and adding a symbol. Use one or two colors for a bigger impact.

What trim would look good on this neckline?

77

Design your own... PANTS

Create your perfect pants by picking a shape and adding cool extras. Start by drawing on these templates and then create your own designs in a sketchbook.

Trims

Add to the waistband or use to decorate the legs.

Pom-poms

Flowers

Patterns

Do you prefer all-over pattern or just in patches?

Experiment with cuffs

Straight leg

My pant shape

What shape do you like the best? What activity would you do in these?

Flares

Formal

Baggy

Cargo

Skinny

Copy these shapes into your sketchbook, then add colors and patterns.

Pick any color

Colorful pants make a fashion statement.

Front

Drawing jeans

To make your drawings look like real jeans, use the right details. Color the jeans blue and draw rivets on the pockets.

You can add some rips and tears.

Include a wide or skinny belt.

Back

Add patches

Design patches inspired by your favorite things.

Design your own... SKIRT

Try out these skirt templates. Once you've chosen a shape, add colors and patterns. What interesting details can you add?

Flowing

Would you wear this skirt to the park or a party?

Invent a fabric

Create a crazy pattern for your skirt (see pages 20–21 for ideas). What pattern works best on a flowing skirt? A tailored one?

Draw on a contrasting seam

Do you want buttons?

Tailored

Pick a pocket

Do you like big or small pockets? Add one to your design.

Could you add a trim to the waistband?

Draw a design on the doll

Add some gorgeous hair and skin color.

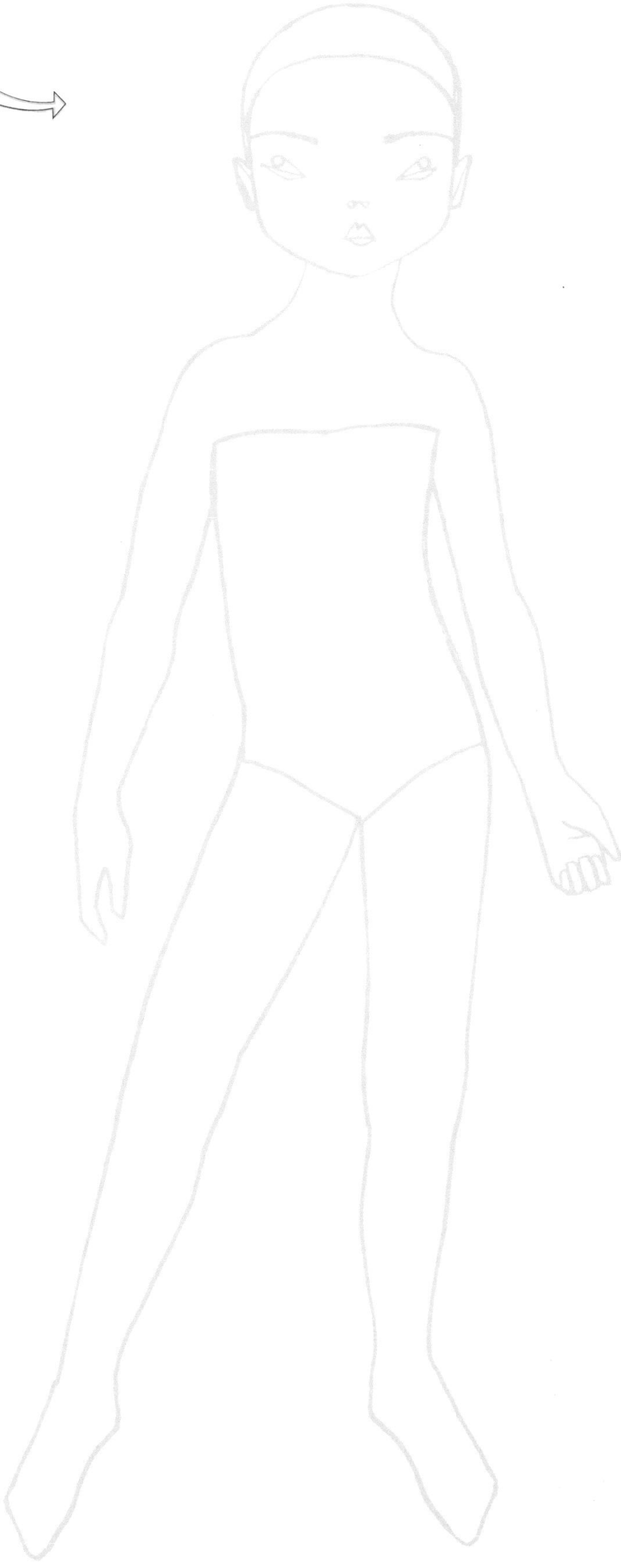

Skater

What top goes best with your skirt?

Design maxi, mini, and knee-length skirts in your sketchbook.

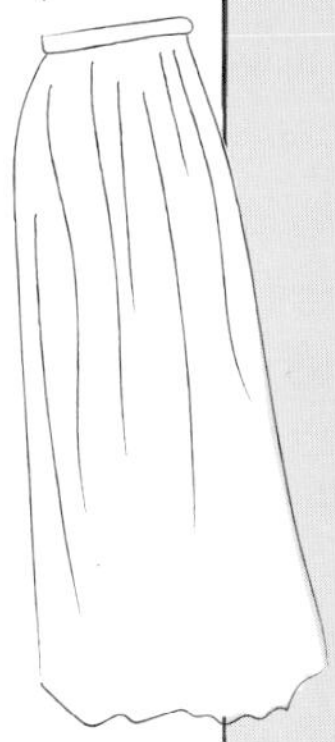

Maxi

Try mixing two different lengths on the same skirt.

Add a pair of shoes to complete the look.

Ballerina

Design your own... NECKLACE

Necklaces can be tiny and delicate or large and chunky.
Try drawing yourself a nameplate necklace or design
a pendant hanging from a chain in any shape you like.

Draw rows of sequins or beads to design a necklace.

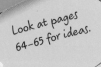

Look at pages 64–65 for ideas.

Test out your design on the doll

Choose sparkling gems
or chunky plastic

Design your own... HAT

Hats and headdresses are the ultimate way to top off an outfit. Whether you like snuggly beanies or fabulous, wide-brimmed summer hats, doodle all your ideas here.

Check out the hat styles on pages 40–41 for ideas.

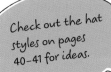

Where would you wear your hat?

Is your hat for winter or summer?

Add some crazy feathers and ribbons.

We need to carry our stuff around and sometimes a pocket just isn't big enough! From your sketchbook and pens to a spare sweater, design a bag that will fit everything you need for the day.

What would you carry in your bag?

Design an inside pocket and lining for your bag.

How does your bag stay closed?

Look at the bag shapes on pages 24–25 for ideas.

Zip

Buttons

Design your own... SHOES

Shoes are made up of the sole on the bottom, the main body of the shoe, and the laces or straps that keep them on your feet. Test out designs on this template, then draw your own shoes.

Try different colors on the sole and body.

Design a pattern for the main body of the shoe.

Add a big bow or a dangling tassel to the laces.

Draw some summery sandals (see page 34).

Design a pair of cozy winter boots.

Tassels

Buckle

Design your own... DRESS

A dress can be sporty and casual or formal and flouncy. Try your hand at designing a dress for a day out and one for a party. What makes them different? How would it feel to wear them?

What shape is your dress?

Write down a texture and a color to inspire your dress.

Draw a dream dress

What length is your dress?

Dress to impress

Draw an amazing dress on the doll

What fabric would your dress be made from? Imagine denim or stretchy cotton. How will this change the design?

Does your dress have short or long sleeves?

Add some sparkle with a necklace.

Add shoes to create a whole outfit.

Design a... PERFECT OUTFIT

You've designed everything from tops to skirts, now put them together to create an amazing outfit that reflects your unique style.

Start by creating a palette of your favorite colors.

Create a mood board to inspire the look of your outfit.

Where will you wear this outfit?

Is your style simple and chic?

Or bold and outrageous?

Top it off with a hat or a headband.

Design an outfit for your perfect day out.

Is your outfit for a sunny or rainy day?

Use thick and thin markers to create bolder or more delicate details.

Shorts, skirts, pants, dresses, jumpsuits, jeans, T-shirts, or blouses? Mix them together to draw the outfits of your dreams.

Take a look back through the book if you need inspiration.

Add a coat or jacket as a finishing touch. Check out pages 68–69 for coat ideas.

Let your imagination run wild

Try top-heavy and bottom-heavy outlines.

What's your inspiration?

Practice outlines before drawing them on the doll (see pages 26–27 for basic silhouettes).

Try the same design in your sketchbook using different colors (look at pages 10–11 for color ideas).

Add accessories to your outfit.

Use metallic marker pens to add sparkling details.

Add pockets and buttons to make your outfit more realistic.

Talk like a
FASHION DESIGNER

Designers use special words and phrases to talk about their creations. Read on to learn how to talk like a fashion designer.

Accessory

Extra item, like a necklace or bag, that can be worn with an outfit

Brand

Line of fashion products under one name

Chic

Another word for "stylish"

Color-blocking

Wearing one or more blocks of solid color in a single outfit

DIY

Stands for "do it yourself"

Dyeing

Using a dye to change the color of a fabric

Embellish

Adding decoration to something

Eyewear

Fashionable glasses or sunglasses

Fashion designer

Person whose job is to come up with ideas for new clothes

Fibers

Very fine threads that make up a material

Fray

Where fabric has been worn away

Garments

Another word for clothes

Headwear

Accessory that is worn on your head, such as a hat, headband, or tiara

Hemline

Folded or sewn edge of a piece of clothing

Inspiration

Something or someone that gives you ideas

Makeover

When you change your clothes or the way you look to try out a new style

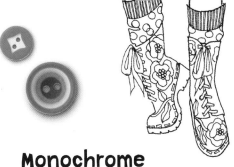

Monochrome
Made up of one color

Mood board
Board of colors, textures, pictures, and objects to give you inspiration

Natural
Natural materials are made from plant and animal fibers such as cotton and wool

Outline
Shape made by the edge of an outfit

Palette
Range of colors and tones that you use in your designs

Pastels
Soft shade of color, such as lilac or baby pink

Pattern
Design that is repeated lots of times

Recycle
Use something instead of throwing it away

Silhouette
See **outline**

Sleepwear
Clothes that you wear to bed

Style
Overall look created by putting together clothes and accessories

Stylist
Person whose job is to put clothing and accessories together

Sustainable fashion
Clothes and accessories made without harming the environment or the people who make them

Swatch
Small piece of fabric

Synthetic
Materials that are made from chemicals by people

Texture
The way a material feels

Trend
Look or outfit that is in fashion at a particular time

Trims
Decorations that are used to make something look nicer

Upcycle
Improve something that you would normally throw away, so that it can be used again

Vintage
Fashion from past decades, such as the 1980s

Volume
Amount of space that a piece of clothing takes up

Wardrobe
Entire collection of clothes

INDEX

ACKNOWLEDGMENTS

The publisher would like to thank: Lol Johnson for photography; Richard Leeney for photography; Belle Thackray and Issy Thomson for modeling and giving interviews; Yumiko Tahata and Maria Thomson for photoshoot assistance; Bettie Capstick, Lola Capstick, Tea Cruz, Chloe Alyse Hadley, and Be Lily Hill for modeling; Jemma Battaglia and Nicola Orme at Alison Hayes for supplying samples; Molly Lattin for additional illustration; Claire Sipi for the index.

Lesley Ware would like to thank her mom and dad, Gwendolyn and the late Herbert Leslie Williams, for having such cool style to admire. She would like to thank the talented and expeditious team at DK Books! Especially Sarah Larter, Satu Fox, Joanne Clark, and Emma Hobson, with whom she had the pleasure of working the most. Also, Tiki Papier for gracing these pages with the World's Most Fashionable Paper Doll!

The publisher would like to thank the following for their kind permission to reproduce their photographs:

(Key: a-above; b-below/bottom; c-center; f-far; l-left; r-right; t-top)

2-3 123RF.com: Natalia Petrova / artnata (b/glitter). **2 123RF.com:** Natalia Petrova / artnata (tc). **Dorling Kindersley:** Natural History Museum, London (tr). **4 Eli Dagostino:** (tr, bl) **8 Getty Images:** Image by Catherine MacBride (tr). **8-9 Getty Images:** Daniel Zuchnik (cb). **9 Alamy Stock Photo:** Gina Easley (crb). **Getty Images:** Tracy Packer (cb). **12 123RF.com:** Edlefler (cl); Moise Marius Dorin (bc); Glebstock (br). **Dreamstime.com:** (cla). **12-13 Dreamstime.com:** Burlesck (c). **28 123RF.com:** Frannyanne (tl); Ruth Black (bl, bc); Michal Vitek (bc/Candies). **28-29 123RF.com:** Amarosy (cb); Grafner (t). **29 123RF.com:** Amarosy (bl). **36 123RF.com:** Petra Schüller / pixelelfe (bc); Sergey Novikov (tl). **Alamy Stock Photo:** Feng Yu (cb); Miscellaneoustock (clb). **37 Dreamstime.com:** Ukrphoto (cla). **40 123RF.com:** vitalily73 (cl). **Alamy Stock Photo:** Image Source (bc). **Dreamstime.com:** Lepas (clb). **40-41 Getty Images:** Naila Ruechel (b). **44 123RF.com:** Marigranula (fbl). **Dreamstime.com:** Oleksiy Maksymenko / Alexmax (tl). **45 123RF.com:** Roman Samokhin (clb). **54 123RF.com:** isselee (bc). **Fotolia:** Eric Isselee (bc/Puppy); Jan Will (bl). **54-55 Dreamstime.com:** Stephanie Berg (t). **58 123RF.com:** Alex Kalmbach (bl); Elena Vagengeim (tl); Pockygallery (cla); Iryna Denysova (ca); Terriana (Music notes). **58-59 123RF.com:** Olaf Herschbach (b). **Dreamstime.com:** Vsg Art Stock Photography And Paintings (cb). **60 Dreamstime.com:** Aleksey Boldin / Apple and iPhone are trademarks of Apple Inc., registered in the U.S. and other countries (bl). **61 123RF.com:** Nina Demianenko (br).

62 123RF.com: Natalia Petrova / artnata (bl/glitter). **Dreamstime.com:** Ambientideas (tl). **63 123RF.com:** Natalia Petrova / artnata (br/glitter). **Dreamstime.com:** Ambientideas (clb, tr). **64 123RF.com:** Laurent Renault (fcra). **Alamy Stock Photo:** Hugh Threlfall (tc). **Dorling Kindersley:** Natural History Museum (cra); Natural History Museum, London (cra/Sapphire). **Dreamstime.com:** Konstantin Kirillov (cl). **64-65 Depositphotos Inc:** Balakleypb (c). **Dorling Kindersley:** Natural History Museum (ca, tc). **65 Dorling Kindersley:** Natural History Museum, London (cla/topaz, ca). **66 Alamy Stock Photo:** J Marshall - Tribaleye Images (tl). **Dorling Kindersley:** Cairo Museum (bl); Gary Ombler / University of Pennsylvania Museum of Archaeology and Anthropology (tc); Ure Museum of Greek Archaeology, University of Reading (cb). **Getty Images:** DEA / S. Vannini / De Agostini (bl/Pectoral). **66-67 Alamy Stock Photo:** Heritage Image Partnership Ltd (c). **Dorling Kindersley:** Cairo Museum (b). **70 Cassie Wagler:** (cr). **Getty Images:** Carol Yepes (br). iStockphoto.com: Podulka (cra). **71 Cassie Wagler:** (clb, bc). **Getty Images:** Juan Jimenez / EyeEm (cl). **72 123RF.com:** Nazarnj (cla). **Dreamstime.com:** Guy Sagi / Gsagi13 (bl); Igor Korionov (tl); Mustafanc (clb); Kati Molin / Molka (br). **72-73 123RF.com:** Bernd Schmidt (tl). **92 123RF.com:** Nina Demianenko (bc). **Dreamstime.com:** Guy Sagi / Gsagi13 (bl)

All other images © Dorling Kindersley
For further information see:
www.dkimages.com

About the illustrator

Tiki Papier is drawn to adventure. An avid illustrator and amateur fashionista, she travels the world with her sidekick, The World's Most Fashionable Paper Doll.

On each trip, Tiki packs an enormous box of pens and a pair of tiny scissors to make new outfits for the ever-changing, ever-stylish paper doll. From Mexico City to Paris to the corner shop, Tiki finds a world of inspiration!